100

MORE

WORDS
every high school graduate should know

THE **100** WORDS   *From the Editors of the*
AMERICAN HERITAGE®
DICTIONARIES

HOUGHTON MIFFLIN HARCOURT

Boston   New York

EDITORIAL STAFF OF THE
American Heritage® Dictionaries

BRUCE NICHOLS, *Senior Vice President, Publisher, Adult Trade and Reference*

STEVEN R. KLEINEDLER, *Executive Editor*

LOUISE E. ROBBINS, *Senior Editor*

PETER CHIPMAN, *Editor*

KATHERINE M. ISAACS, *Consulting Editor*

CHRISTOPHER J. GRANNISS, *Database Production Supervisor*

MARGARET ANNE MILES, *Art and Production Supervisor*

SARAH IANI, *Associate Production Editor*

LIBRARY OF CONGRESS CATALOGING-IN-PUBLICATION DATA
100 more words every high school graduate should know / from
the Editors of the American Heritage Dictionaries.
p. cm. — ([100 words series])
ISBN 978-0-544-01966-9
1. Vocabulary. I. Title: One hundred more words every
high school graduate should know.
PE1449.A1424 2013
413 — dc23
2012030710

MANUFACTURED IN THE UNITED STATES OF AMERICA

1 2 3 4 5 6 7 8 9 10 - DOC - 18 17 16 15 14 13

Table of Contents

Preface

In the past ten years, the editors of the American Heritage Dictionaries have published a dozen titles in the *100 Words* series, including *100 Words Every High School Graduate Should Know*, *100 Words Almost Everyone Confuses and Misuses*, and *100 Words to Make You Sound Smart*. The response has been tremendous—over 750,000 copies have been sold, and we have received a great deal of positive feedback.

These books are intended to foster a love of language and to generate interest in dictionaries. Each title stands on its own, but in each case, we have hoped that the words selected would spur readers to explore the English language in greater depth. The full richness of the language is available at your fingertips in *The American Heritage Dictionary of the English Language*, Fifth Edition, available in print, as an app, or online at ahdictionary.com. We are encouraged to see that so many people are aware of the importance of dictionaries for promoting literacy and vocabulary building.

Our readers have let us know that they enjoy a challenge, and we are happy to oblige with our newest title, *100 More Words Every High School Graduate Should Know*, a balanced mix of essential words from A through Z. We have chosen vocabulary items that can be found on standardized tests, such as *nascence, querulous,* and *verisimilitude,* along with a selection of words that students should be familiar with from their studies, such as *caldera, hydrocarbon,* and *oviparous.* Numerous example sentences and quotations show the use of the entry words in context. Knowledge of these words will help students and adults alike build a more sophisticated vocabulary.

We hope that you find learning these words and expanding your vocabulary to be a rewarding experience.

—Steve Kleinedler
Executive Editor

Guide to the Entries

ENTRY WORD The 100 words that constitute this book are listed alphabetically. The entry words, along with inflected and derived forms, are divided into syllables by centered dots. These dots show you where you would break the word at the end of a line. The pronunciation of the word follows the entry word. The information and chart on pages viii and ix explain the pronunciation system.

PART OF SPEECH At least one part of speech follows each entry word. The part of speech tells you the grammatical category that the word belongs to. Parts of speech appearing in this book include *noun, adjective, adverb, transitive verb,* and *intransitive verb.* (A transitive verb is a verb whose meaning is completed by a direct object. *Wash* is transitive in the sentence *I washed the car.* The direct object of *wash* is *the car.* An intransitive verb is one that does not take an object, such as *sleep* in the sentence *I slept for seven hours.* Many verbs are both transitive and intransitive.)

INFLECTIONS A word's inflected form differs from the main entry form by the addition of a suffix or by a change in its base form to indicate grammatical features such as number, person, or tense. The past tense, past participle, and the third person singular present tense inflections of all verbs are shown. The plurals of nouns are shown when they are spelled in a way other than by adding *s* to the base form.

LABELS A subject label identifies the special area of knowledge a definition applies to, as at *derivative,* which has specific linguistics, mathematics, and chemistry senses.

ORDER OF SENSES Entries having more than one sense are arranged with the central and often the most commonly sought meanings first. Senses and subsenses are grouped to show their relationships with each other. Boldface letters before senses indicate that two or more subsenses are closely related, as at *nominal.*

EXAMPLES OF USAGE Examples often follow the definitions and are set in italic type. These examples show the entry words in typical contexts. Sometimes the examples are quotations from books or newspaper articles. These examples are shown within quotation marks, and the quotation's author and source are shown.

ETYMOLOGIES Etymologies appear in square brackets following the last definition. An etymology traces the history of a word. The stage most closely preceding Modern English is given first, with each earlier stage following in sequence. A language name, linguistic form (in italics), and brief definition of the form are given for each stage of the derivation. Occasionally, a form will be given that is not actually preserved in written documents but which scholars are confident did exist—such a form will be marked by an asterisk (*). The word "from" is used to indicate origin of any kind: by inheritance, borrowing, or derivation. When an etymology splits a compound word into parts, a colon introduces the parts and each element is then traced back to its origin, with those elements enclosed in parentheses.

RELATED WORDS At the end of many entries, additional boldface words appear without definitions. These words are related in basic meaning to the entry word and are usually formed from the entry word by the addition of suffixes.

WORD HISTORY NOTES Word Histories are found at words whose etymologies are of particular interest. The bare facts of the etymology are explained to give a fuller understanding of how important linguistic processes operate, how words move from one language to another, and how the history of an individual word can be related to historical and cultural developments.

Pronunciation Guide

Pronunciations appear in parentheses after boldface entry words. If a word has more than one pronunciation, the first pronunciation is usually more common than the other, but often they are equally common. Pronunciations are shown after inflections and related words where necessary.

Stress is the relative degree of emphasis that a word's syllables are spoken with. An unmarked syllable has the weakest stress in the word. The strongest, or primary, stress is indicated with a bold mark (ʹ). A lighter mark (ʹ) indicates a secondary level of stress. The stress mark follows the syllable it applies to. Words of one syllable have no stress mark because there is no other stress level that the syllable can be compared to.

The key on page ix shows the pronunciation symbols used in this book. To the right of the symbols are words that show how the symbols are pronounced. The letters whose sound corresponds to the symbols are shown in boldface.

The symbol (ə) is called *schwa*. It represents a vowel with the weakest level of stress in a word. The schwa sound varies slightly according to the vowel it represents or the sounds around it:

a·bun·dant (ə-bŭnʹdənt)   **mo·ment** (mōʹmənt)
civ·il (sĭvʹəl)   **grate·ful** (grātʹfəl)

PRONUNCIATION KEY

Symbol	Examples	Symbol	Examples
ă	pat	oi	noise
ā	pay	o͝o	took
âr	care	o͝or	lure
ä	father	o͞o	boot
b	bib	ou	out
ch	church	p	pop
d	deed, milled	r	roar
ĕ	pet	s	sauce
ē	bee	sh	ship, dish
f	fife, phase, rough	t	tight, stopped
		th	thin
g	gag	*th*	this
h	hat	ŭ	cut
hw	which	ûr	urge, term, firm, word, heard
ĭ	pit		
ī	pie, by		
îr	deer, pier	v	valve
j	judge	w	with
k	kick, cat, pique	y	yes
l	lid, needle	z	zebra, xylem
m	mum	zh	vision, pleasure, garage
n	no, sudden		
ng	thing		
ŏ	pot	ə	about, item, edible, gallop, circus
ō	toe		
ô	caught, paw		
ôr	core	ər	butter

The final act [of the opera] was more astounding than the first. I knew now that the actors were not wholly involved in their roles because I had seen the **alacrity** with which they shuffled off their characters, and yet they caught me again and wove me deftly into the pattern of the play.

—Maya Angelou
*Singin' and Swingin' and
Gettin' Merry Like Christmas*

a·lac·ri·ty (ə-lăk′rĭ-tē)

noun

1. Speed or quickness: *"I knew now that the actors were not wholly involved in their roles because I had seen the alacrity with which they shuffled off their characters"* (Maya Angelou, *Singin' and Swingin' and Gettin' Merry Like Christmas*). **2.** Cheerful willingness; eagerness: *They approached the difficult task with alacrity.*

[Latin *alacritās*, from *alacer*, lively.]

RELATED WORD:
    adjective—**a·lac′ri·tous** (ə-lăk′rĭ-təs)

a·mor·phous (ə-môr′fəs)

adjective

1. Lacking physical form or shape. **2.** Lacking organization; formless: *"He helped me turn a deeply felt but amorphous idea into a coherent narrative"* (James S. Hirsch, *Cheating Destiny*). **3.** Lacking a crystalline structure: *Glass is an amorphous material.*

[From Greek *amorphos* : *a-*, without + *morphē*, shape.]

RELATED WORDS:
    adverb—**a·mor′phous·ly**
    noun—**a·mor′phous·ness**

3

a·nath·e·ma (ə-năth′ə-mə)

noun

1. A person or thing that is intensely disliked: *The idea of giving up before the end of the race was anathema to her.* **2.** A strong denunciation or condemnation; a curse: *"the sound of a witch's anathemas in some unknown tongue"* (Nathaniel Hawthorne, *The Scarlet Letter*). **3.** A formal ban or excommunication imposed by a church.

[Late Latin, doomed offering, accursed thing, from Greek, from *anatithenai, anathe-*, to dedicate : *ana-*, upward + *tithenai*, to put.]

4

an·o·mie (ăn′ə-mē)

noun

1. Alienation and purposelessness experienced by a person or a class as a result of a lack of standards, values, or ideals: *a novel about a troubled teenager suffering from boredom and anomie.* **2.** Social instability caused by erosion of standards and values: *Rapid growth in the economy led to anomie.*

[French, from Greek *anomiā*, lawlessness, from *anomos*, lawless : *a-*, without + *nomos*, law.]

5

an·tith·e·sis (ăn-tĭth′ĭ-sĭs)

noun
    Plural: **an·tith·e·ses** (ăn-tĭth′ĭ-sēz′)

1. Direct contrast; opposition: *Your behavior stands in antithesis to your beliefs.* **2.** The direct or exact opposite: *Hope is the antithesis of despair.* **3a.** A figure of speech in which sharply contrasting ideas are juxtaposed in a balanced or parallel phrase or grammatical structure, as in *"It was the best of times, it was the worst of times"* (Charles Dickens, *A Tale of Two Cities*). **b.** The second and contrasting part of such a juxtaposition. **4.** A stage following and standing in opposition to the thesis, in German philosopher Georg Hegel's theory of intellectual and historical development.

[Late Latin, from Greek, from *antitithenai*, *antithe-*, to oppose : *anti-*, opposite + *tithenai*, to put.]

6

a·poth·e·o·sis (ə-pŏth′ē-ō′sĭs)

noun

    Plural: **a·poth·e·o·ses** (ə-pŏth′ē-ō′sēz′)

1. The elevation to divine rank or status; deification: *the apotheosis of a Roman emperor.* **2.** Elevation to an exalted or glorified position: *"tried to attribute [Andy] Warhol's current apotheosis to the subversive power of artistic vision"* (Michiko Kakutani, *New York Times Magazine*). **3.** An exalted or glorified example: *Their leader was the apotheosis of courage.*

[Late Latin *apotheōsis*, from Greek, from *apotheoun*, to deify : *apo-*, change + *theos*, god.]

7

ar·ca·num (är-kā′nəm)

noun

    Plural: **ar·ca·na** (är-kā′nə) or **ar·ca·nums**

1. A deep secret; a mystery: *The origin of this custom is an arcanum known only to a few.* **2. arcana** Specialized knowledge or detail that is mysterious to the average person: *"knows the arcana of police procedure and the intricacies of litigation"* (George F. Will, "Cast Politics Aside and Read a Good Book").

[Latin *arcānum*, from neuter of *arcānus* secret.]

8

ba·thos (bā′thŏs′)

noun

1. A sudden change from a dignified or serious style to one that is very commonplace, producing a ridiculous effect. **2.** Insincere or grossly sentimental pathos: *"a richly textured man who, at 53, can be . . . sentimental to the brink of bathos"* (Kenneth L. Woodward, *Newsweek*). **3.** Banality; triteness.

[Greek *bathos*, depth, from *bathus*, deep.]

9

bell·weth·er (bĕl′wĕth′ər)

noun

One that serves as a leader or as a leading indicator of future trends: *"The degree to which the paper is censored is a political bellwether"* (Justine De Lacy, *The Atlantic*).

[Middle English *bellewether*, wether (a castrated male sheep or goat) with a bell hung from its neck, leader of the flock.]

be·speak (bĭ-spēk′)

transitive verb
> Past tense: **be·spoke** (bĭ-spōk′)
> Past participle: **be·spo·ken** (bĭ-spō′kən) or **be·spoke**
> Present participle: **be·speak·ing**
> Third person singular present tense: **be·speaks**

1a. To be or give a sign of; indicate: *"Their impeccable coiffures bespoke a recent trip to the beauty parlor"* (Daniel B. Silver, *Refuge in Hell*). **b.** To foretell; portend: *"He salutes them with a stricken look, as if their arrival bespeaks doom for him"* (Edna O'Brien, *In the Forest*). **2a.** To engage, hire, or order in advance: *He wrote to the innkeeper to bespeak a room for the week.* **b.** To request: *bespeak a favor.* **3.** *Archaic* To speak to; address.

[Middle English *bispeken*, to speak out, from Old English *besprecan*, to speak about.]

"I'm her sister ... I'm desperate ... my mother and father are desperate ... put yourself in our position ... help us."

"I can't," Mrs. Rafferty says, retreating backwards into the house and almost colliding with her husband, who has obviously been listening. He salutes them with a stricken look, as if their arrival **bespeaks** doom for him. He speaks rapidly, as if in a witness box, giving a prepared statement: "I saw her drive past here at approximately twelve noon last Friday. There was a man in the back aged about twenty with dark brown hair and he had on a green jacket."

—Edna O'Brien
In the Forest

cal·de·ra (kăl-dâr′ə, käl-dâr′ə)

noun

A large crater formed by volcanic explosion or by collapse of a volcanic cone.

[Spanish, cauldron, caldera, from Late Latin *caldāria*.]

🐚 **WORD HISTORY Caldera** means "cauldron" in Spanish, and by extension, the Spanish word was applied to volcanic craters, in which steaming lakes of sulfurous water or even pits of bubbling lava can sometimes be seen. *Caldera* first began to be used in English in the 1600s. The Spanish word *caldera* comes from Latin *caldāria*, "pot for boiling," and *caldāria* is in origin the feminine of the Latin adjective *caldārius*, "suitable for warming." *Caldārius* is itself derived from the Latin adjective *calidus*, "warm." *Calidus* is also the source of the Spanish word *caldo*, "broth"—from an etymological point of view, *caldo* is simply "the warm stuff." Spanish *caldera* has a surprising relative in English: *chowder*. In the dialects of central France, where Latin *c* had become *ch* before *a*, Latin *caldāria*, "pot for boiling," became *chaudière*. French fishermen brought this word to Newfoundland, Quebec, and Acadia when they settled these areas in the 1600s, and since the sea was a chief source of sustenance for the coastal French colonies, the *chaudière* simmering in their kitchens usually contained cod or clams. By the middle of the 1700s, *chaudière* had spread into the kitchens of English-speaking Newfoundlanders and New Englanders as the word for thick seafood soup, *chowder*.

co·a·lesce (kō'ə-lĕs')

intransitive verb

Past participle and past tense: **co·a·lesced**

Present participle: **co·a·lesc·ing**

Third person singular present tense: **co·a·lesc·es**

1. To come or grow together into a single mass: *the material that coalesced to form stars.* **2.** To come together as a recognizable whole or entity: *the stories that coalesced as the history of the movement.* **3.** To come together for a single purpose: *The rebel units coalesced into one army to fight the invaders.*

[Latin *coalēscere* : *co-*, together + *alēscere*, to grow.]

RELATED WORDS:

noun — **co'a·les'cence**

adjective — **co'a·les'cent**

com·punc·tion (kəm-pŭngk′shən)

noun

A sting of conscience or feeling of uneasiness about something one has done or contemplates doing: *"Some journalists have no compunction about printing or broadcasting controversial news about a political candidate in the last weeks of an election campaign"* (Jacques Steinberg and David Carr, *New York Times*).

[Middle English *compunccioun*, from Old French *componction*, from Late Latin *compūnctiō*, *compūnctiōn-*, puncture, sting of conscience, from Latin *compūnctus*, past participle of *compungere*, to sting.]

RELATED WORDS:
> *adjective* — **com·punc′tious** (kəm-pŭngk′-
>> shəs)
> *adverb* — **com·punc′tious·ly**

con·flate (kən-flāt′)

transitive verb
> Past participle and past tense: **con·flat·ed**
> Present participle: **con·flat·ing**
> Third person singular present tense: **con·flates**

1. To treat or present (two or more distinct things) as the same thing: *"The problems* [with the biopic] *include . . . dates moved around, lovers deleted, many characters conflated into one"* (Ty Burr, *Entertainment Weekly*). **2.** To combine (two variant texts, for example) into one whole.

[Latin *cōnflāre, cōnflāt-* : *com-*, together + *flāre*, to blow.]

RELATED WORD:
> *noun* — **con·fla′tion**

cre·pus·cu·lar (krĭ-pŭs′kyə-lər)

adjective

1. Relating to or like twilight; dim: *the castle's crepuscular halls.* **2a.** Active primarily at dawn or dusk or both. Used of animals: *crepuscular bees.* **b.** Occurring at dawn or dusk or both: *crepuscular foraging; a crepuscular stroll through the park.*

[From Latin *crepusculum*, twilight, from Latin *creper*, dark.]

cy·no·sure (sī′nə-sho͝or′, sĭn′ə-sho͝or′)

noun

1. A center of attention or interest: *The famous movie star was the cynosure of all eyes when he entered the restaurant.* **2.** Something that serves to guide.

[French, Ursa Minor (which contains the guiding star Polaris), from Latin *cynosūra*, from Greek *kunosoura*, dog's tail, Ursa Minor : *kunos*, genitive of *kuōn*, dog + *ourā*, tail.]

RELATED WORD:

    adjective **— cy′no·sur′al**

🐾 **WORD HISTORY** Cynosure first appeared in English as a name for the constellation Ursa Minor (the Little Dipper), a star formation that was once noted for its use in locating the celestial north pole—the axis around which all the constellations of the Northern Hemisphere rotate. The last star in the handle of the "dipper," or ladle, is Polaris, which, because of its proximity to the pole, also goes by the names *polestar* and *North Star*. Polaris's relatively constant position in the north sky has made it an important beacon for celestial navigators and a wellspring of metaphors for poets. According to ancient sources, the practice of using Ursa Minor to locate the star originated in Phoenicia, an ancient maritime country of southwest Asia. The word *cynosure* itself can be traced back to one of the early representations of Ursa Minor. The word's Greek ancestor, *kunosoura*, was another name for the constellation Ursa Minor and literally translates as "dog's tail."

de·bunk (dē-bŭngk′)

transitive verb

Past participle and past tense: **de·bunked**
Present participle: **de·bunk·ing**
Third person singular present tense: **de·bunks**

To expose or ridicule the falseness or exaggerated claims of: *Scientists have debunked the theory that baking soda can cure cancer.*

RELATED WORD:
noun — **de·bunk′er**

🖎 **WORD HISTORY** The *bunk* in **debunk** came from a place where much bunk has originated, the United States Congress. During the 16th Congress (1819–1821), Felix Walker, representative from the district in North Carolina including Buncombe County, delivered a particularly pointless speech intended merely to convince his constituents that he was making a difference in Washington. His colleagues asked him to stop, but he nattered on despite their protests—he was speaking not to Congress, he explained, but "to Buncombe." *Buncombe,* respelled *bunkum* and later shortened to *bunk,* thus became synonymous with "nonsense." In 1923, the writer William E. Woodward coined the term *debunk* by adding the prefix *de-,* "to remove," to the word *bunk.*

de·riv·a·tive (dĭ-rĭv′ə-tĭv)

adjective

1. Produced by adapting or altering something else: *English has many derivative words.* **2.** Lacking in originality: *a highly derivative prose style.*

noun

1. Something that is derived: *a martial art that is a derivative of karate.* **2.** *Linguistics* A word formed by altering a preexisting word, such as *electricity* from *electric.* **3.** *Mathematics* In calculus, the slope of the tangent line to a curve at a particular point on the curve. When a curve represents a function with x as the independent variable and y as the dependent variable, its derivative can also be thought of as the rate of change of the corresponding function at the given point. Derivatives are computed using differentiation. **4.** *Chemistry* A compound derived or obtained from another and containing essential elements of the parent substance. **5.** A financial instrument that derives its value from another more fundamental asset, as a commitment to buy a bond for a certain sum on a certain date.

[From French *dérivatif.*]

RELATED WORD:
    adverb—**de·riv′a·tive·ly**

19

di·aph·a·nous (dī-ăf′ə-nəs)

adjective

1. So fine or gauzy that light can pass through: *a diaphanous curtain; a robe made of diaphanous fabric.* **2.** Delicate and insubstantial: *diaphanous butterfly wings.*

[From Medieval Latin *diaphanus*, transparent, from Greek *diaphanēs*, from *diaphainein*, to be transparent : *dia-*, through + *phainein*, *phan-*, to show.]

RELATED WORD:
    adverb —**di·aph′a·nous·ly**

20

du·ress (dŏŏ-rĕs′)

noun

1. The use of force or threat to compel someone to do something: *The prisoner confessed under duress.* **2.** Constraint or difficulty caused by misfortune: *"children who needed only temporary care because their parents were ill, out of work, or under some other form of duress"* (Stephen O'Connor, *Orphan Trains*). **3.** Forcible confinement.

[Middle English *duresse*, harshness, compulsion, from Old French *durece*, hardness, from Latin *dūritia*, from *dūrus*, hard.]

ef·face (ĭ-fās′)

transitive verb

Past participle and past tense: **ef·faced**
Present participle: **ef·fac·ing**
Third person singular present tense: **ef·fac·es**

1. To remove, as by rubbing out; erase: *Years of harsh weather had effaced the name on the gravestone. The forger had effaced the original signature and replaced it with his own.* **2.** To conduct (oneself) inconspicuously: *"When the two women went out together, Anna deliberately effaced herself and played to the dramatic Molly"* (Doris Lessing, *The Golden Notebook*).

[Middle English *effacen*, from French *effacer*, from Old French *esfacier* : *es-*, out (from Latin *ex-*, out) + *face*, face.]

RELATED WORDS:
adjective—**ef·face′a·ble**
noun—**ef·face′ment**
noun—**ef·fac′er**

When the two women went out together, Anna deliberately **effaced** herself and played to the dramatic Molly. When they were alone, she tended to take the lead. But this by no means had been true at the beginning of their friendship. Molly, abrupt, straightforward, tactless, had frankly domineered Anna. Slowly … Anna learned to stand up for herself.

—Doris Lessing
The Golden Notebook

ef·ful·gent (ĭ-fo͝ol′jənt, ĭ-fŭl′jənt)

adjective

1. Shining brilliantly; resplendent: *an effulgent tiara.* **2.** Showing or expressing vitality, love, or joy: *"the thrilling promise he held out in his effulgent emerald eyes"* (Arundhati Roy, *The God of Small Things*).

[Latin *effulgēns, effulgent-*, present participle of *effulgēre,* to shine out : *ex-*, out of + *fulgēre,* to shine.]

e·pon·y·mous (ĭ-pŏn′ə-məs)

adjective

Named after something else or deriving from an existing name or word: *"Programs such as He-Man and Masters of the Universe . . . were all created with the explicit purpose of selling the eponymous toys to children"* (Susan Gregory Thomas, *Buy, Buy Baby*).

[From Greek *epōnumos.*]

eu·re·ka (yŏo-rē′kə)

interjection

An expression used to express triumph upon discovering something or finding a solution to a problem.

[Greek *heurēka,* I have found (it) (supposedly exclaimed by Archimedes upon discovering how to measure the volume of an irregular solid and thereby determine the purity of a gold object), first person singular perfect tense of *heuriskein,* to find.]

ex·co·ri·ate (ĭk-skôr′ē-āt′)

transitive verb
> Past participle and past tense: **ex·co·ri·at·ed**
> Present participle: **ex·co·ri·at·ing**
> Third person singular present tense: **ex·co·ri·ates**

1. To censure (someone) strongly: denounce: *The judge excoriated the reporter for leaking details of the case.* **2.** To criticize (something) harshly: *"After excoriating the vapid culture of movie-star worship . . . he's ended up at that trough"* (Maureen Dowd, *New York Times*). **3.** To tear, scrape, or wear off (the skin).

[Middle English *excoriaten,* from Latin *excoriāre, excoriāt-* : *ex-,* away from, out of + *corium,* skin.]

RELATED WORDS:
> *noun* —**ex·co′ri·a′tion**
> *noun* —**ex·co′ri·a′tor**

I do remember the way that my father would go after our pumpkins, once we got them home, with the biggest knife from the kitchen drawer. He was a **fastidious** man who hated to dirty his hands, in particular with food, but he was also a doctor, and there was something grimly expert about the way he scalped the orange crania, excised the stringy pulp, and scraped clean the pale interior flesh with the edge of a big metal spoon.

—Michael Chabon
Along the Frontage Road

fas·tid·i·ous (fă-stĭd′ē-əs)

adjective

1. Showing or acting with careful attention to detail: *a fastidious scholar; fastidious research.* **2.** Difficult to please; choosy; exacting: *"The club is also becoming far more fastidious about what constitutes a breed standard"* (Janet Burroway, *Bridge of Sand*). **3.** Excessively scrupulous or sensitive, as in taste, propriety, or neatness: *"He was a fastidious man who hated to dirty his hands, in particular with food"* (Michael Chabon, *Along the Frontage Road*). **4.** *Microbiology* Having complex nutritional requirements: *fastidious bacteria.*

[Middle English, squeamish, particular, haughty, from Old French *fastidieux*, from Latin *fastīdiōsus*, from *fastīdium*, squeamishness, haughtiness, probably from *fastus*, disdain.]

RELATED WORDS:
  adverb—**fas·tid′i·ous·ly**
  noun—**fas·tid′i·ous·ness**

feint (fānt)

noun

1. A military attack or maneuver that is meant to divert attention away from a planned point of attack. **2.** A body movement that is intended to divert another's attention, often by being deliberately left uncompleted: *"The mongoose begins with a feint, which provokes the snake to strike"* (Norbert Wiener, *Cybernetics*). **3.** An action meant to mislead: *The robbers made a feint of repairing the window they were going to break into.*

intransitive verb

> Past participle and past tense: **feint·ed**
> Present participle: **feint·ing**
> Third person singular present tense: **feints**

To make a feint: *"He feinted with his left hand, trying to distract the turtle and then grab its tail"* (Howard Frank Mosher, *Waiting for Teddy Williams*).

[French *feinte*, from Old French, from past participle of *feindre*, to feign.]

fe·ral (fîr′əl, fĕr′əl)

adjective

1. Existing in a wild or untamed state, especially after having been domesticated: *feral cats living in the park.*
2. Relating to or suggestive of a wild animal; savage: *a feral grin.*

[From Latin *fera*, wild animal, from *ferus*, wild.]

gaffe (găf)

noun

1. A clumsy social error; a faux pas: *"The excursion had in his eyes been a monstrous gaffe, a breach of sensibility and good taste, for which he would never forgive her"* (Mary McCarthy, *The Company She Keeps*). **2.** A blatant mistake or misjudgment.

[French *gaffe*, from Old French *gaffe*, hook.]

gal·va·nize (găl′və-nīz′)

transitive verb
   Past participle and past tense: **gal·va·nized**
   Present participle: **gal·va·niz·ing**
   Third person singular present tense: **gal·va·niz·es**

1. To coat (iron or steel) with rust-resistant zinc. **2.** To arouse to awareness or action; spur: *"Issues that once galvanized the electorate fade into irrelevance"* (Arthur M. Schlesinger, Jr).

[After Luigi *Galvani* (1737–1798), Italian physiologist.]

RELATED WORDS:
   noun — **gal′va·ni·za′tion** (găl′və-nĭ-zā′shən)
   noun — **gal′va·niz′er**

grav·i·tas (grăv′ĭ-täs′)

noun

Seriousness or solemnity in demeanor or treatment: *a candidate who lacks gravitas; an article with sufficient gravitas to be compelling.*

[Latin *gravitās*, heaviness, seriousness.]

ha·bil·i·ments (hə-bĭl′ə-mənts)

plural noun

Clothing, especially the clothing associated with a special occasion or profession: *"The figure was tall and gaunt, and shrouded from head to foot in the habiliments of the grave"* (Edgar Allan Poe, *The Masque of the Red Death*).

[Middle English *habilement*, from Old French *habillement*, from *habiller*, to clothe, alteration (influenced by *habit*, clothing) of *abiller*, to prepare, strip a tree of its branches : *a-*, toward + *bille*, log.]

The figure was tall and gaunt, and shrouded from head to foot in the **habiliments** of the grave. The mask which concealed the visage was made so nearly to resemble the countenance of a stiffened corpse that the closest scrutiny must have had difficulty in detecting the cheat.

—Edgar Allan Poe
The Masque of the Red Death

het·er·o·dox (hĕt′ər-ə-dŏks′)

adjective

Not in agreement with accepted beliefs, especially in church doctrine or dogma: *a heterodox religious movement; heterodox theories of economic development.*

[Greek *heterodoxos* : *hetero-*, other + *doxa*, opinion (from *dokein*, to think).]

hy·dro·car·bon (hī′drə-kär′bən)

noun

Any of numerous organic compounds, such as benzene and methane, that contain only carbon and hydrogen. Petroleum, for example, is made of a mixture of hydrocarbons.

[*hydr(o)*– (from Greek *hudro-*, *hudr-*, from Greek *hudōr*, water) + *carbon* (from French *carbone*, from Latin *carbō*, *carbōn-*, a coal, charcoal).]

35

im·pugn (ĭm-pyo͞on′)

transitive verb
> Past participle and past tense: **im·pugned**
> Present participle: **im·pugn·ing**
> Third person singular present tense: **im·pugns**

To attack as false or questionable; challenge in argument: *The candidate's speech impugned the record of his opponent.*

[Middle English *impugnen*, from Old French *impugner*, from Latin *impugnāre* : *in-*, against + *pugnāre*, to fight.]

RELATED WORDS:
> *adjective*—**im·pugn′a·ble**
> *noun*—**im·pugn′er**

in·cho·ate (ĭn-kō′ĭt, ĭn-kō′āt′)

adjective

1. Being in a beginning or early stage; incipient: *"The country was developing an incipient national art, an inchoate national literature"* (Jay Winik, *April 1865*). **2.** Imperfectly formed or developed; disordered or incoherent: *"A prophet must be a good public speaker, someone who can transform inchoate rage into eloquent diatribe"* (David Leavitt, *The Marble Quilt*).

[Latin *inchoātus*, past participle of *inchoāre*, to begin, alteration of *incohāre* : *in-*, in + *cohum*, strap from yoke to harness.]

RELATED WORDS:
> *adverb*—**in·cho′ate·ly**
> *noun*—**in·cho′ate·ness**

in·dig·e·nous (ĭn-dĭj′ə-nəs)

adjective

1. Originally living or growing in a particular place or region; native: *The bald eagle is indigenous to North America.* **2a.** Being a member of the original inhabitants of a particular place: *indigenous peoples.* **b.** Relating to, belonging to, or characteristic of such inhabitants: *indigenous customs.*

[From Latin *indigena*, a native.]

RELATED WORD:
> *adverb*—**in·dig′e·nous·ly**

---

in·nate (ĭ-nāt′, ĭn′āt′)

adjective

1a. Existing from birth rather than being learned; inborn: *"Chimpanzees show an innate distrust of contact with strangers"* (Cindy Engel, *Wild Health*). **b.** Relating to or produced by the mind rather than sense experience: *innate ideas about space and time.* **2.** Possessed as an essential characteristic; inherent: *"As the Army [Corps of Engineers] and farmers built more and more levees, the Missouri lost an innate capacity to absorb its frequent excesses"* (William Least Heat-Moon, *River Horse*).

[Middle English *innat*, from Latin *innātus*, past participle of *innāscī*, to be born in : *in-*, in + *nāscī*, to be born.]

RELATED WORDS:

    adverb — **in·nate′ly**
    noun — **in·nate′ness**

in·tran·si·gent (ĭn-trăn′zə-jənt)

adjective

Refusing to moderate a position, especially an extreme position; stubborn: *Both sides remained intransigent, and so no compromise could be reached.*

[French *intransigeant*, from Spanish *intransigente* : *in-*, not (from Latin) + *transigente*, present participle of *transigir*, to compromise (from Latin *trānsigere*, to come to an agreement).]

RELATED WORDS:
> *noun* — in·tran′si·gence, in·tran′si·gen·cy
> *noun* — in·tran′si·gent
> *adverb* — in·tran′si·gent·ly

jug·ger·naut (jŭg′ər-nôt′)

noun

An overwhelming or unstoppable force: *"It doesn't assume that people need necessarily remain passive when confronted by what appears to be the juggernaut of history"* (Christopher Lehmann-Haupt).

[Hindi *jagannāth*, title of Krishna, from Sanskrit *jagannāthaḥ*, lord of the world : *jagat*, moving, the world (from earlier present participle of *jigāti*, he goes) + *nāthaḥ*, lord (from *nāthate*, he helps, protects).]

☙ **WORD HISTORY** For centuries, the Indian city of Puri has held an annual festival in honor of the god Krishna, worshiped under his Sanskrit title *Jagannāthaḥ*, "Lord of the World." In the middle of the rainy season, devotees transport highly adorned

---

figures representing Krishna, his brother Baladeva, and his half-sister Subhadra from the temple where they usually reside to another temple some two and a half miles away. There, Krishna enjoys the new locale until his return a week or two later. Krishna and his siblings are transported in three chariots—massive towerlike structures about 45 feet high, mounted on many wheels, and lavishly decorated. Thousands of devotees pull the chariots with ropes and are cheered on by a crowd of over a million pilgrims. Worshipers try to obtain blessings by touching the ropes, and some have been crushed in the throng or have fallen under the wheels. Early Western observers in colonial India greatly exaggerated the number of these deaths, however, and sensationalized reports of the incidents led to the borrowing of *Jagannāthaḥ* into English as **juggernaut,** "an irresistible force that rolls unstoppably over its victims."

kel·vin (kĕl′vĭn)

noun
Plural: **kelvin**

The unit that is used to measure temperature in the Kelvin scale, a scale of temperature that begins at absolute zero (−273.15°C or −459.67°F) and has units of the same magnitude as those of the Celsius scale. On the Kelvin scale, water freezes at 273.15 K and boils at 373.15 K.

[After First Baron *Kelvin* (1824–1907), British physicist.]

la·cu·na (lə-kyōō′nə, lə-kōō′nə)

noun

Plural: **la·cu·nae** (lə-kyōō′nē) or **la·cu·nas**

1. An empty space or a missing part; a gap: *Even though you have studied music for years, there are some real lacunae in your knowledge.* **2.** *Anatomy* A cavity, space, or depression, especially in a bone.

[Latin *lacūna*, pool, hollow, gap.]

RELATED WORD:
 adjective — **la·cu′nal**

lam·bent (lăm′bənt)

adjective

1. Flickering gently over a surface: *lambent moonlight.* **2.** Having a gentle glow; luminous: *"A lambent moon cast shadows on crumbling walls"* (Stephen Benz, "A Cup of Cuban Coffee"). **3.** Showing effortless brilliance or lightness: *a lambent mind.*

[Latin *lambēns, lambent-,* present participle of *lambere,* to lick.]

RELATED WORDS:
 noun — **lam′ben·cy**
 adverb — **lam′bent·ly**

[Havana] was, I found, a city rich in variations of light: the long morning rays filtering through dust and tropical vegetation; the glare of the midday sun on the city's faded pastels; the chiaroscuro of the evening in the maze of Old Havana where faltering neon and a **lambent** moon cast shadows on crumbling walls.

—Stephen Benz
"A Cup of Cuban Coffee"

lin·e·a·ment (lĭn′ē-ə-mənt)

noun

1. A distinctive shape, contour, or line, especially of the face. **2.** often **lineaments** A definitive or characteristic feature: *"the gross and subtle folds of corruption on the average senatorial face are hardly the lineaments of virtue"* (Norman Mailer, *Vanity Fair*).

[Middle English *liniament*, from Latin *līneāmentum*, from *līnea*, line.]

Lud·dite (lŭd′īt)

noun

1. Any of a group of British workers who between 1811 and 1816 rioted and destroyed labor-saving textile machinery in the belief that such machinery would diminish employment. **2.** A person who opposes technical or technological change: *They accused me of being a Luddite when I said I didn't like to read e-books.*

[After Ned *Ludd*, an English laborer who was supposed to have destroyed weaving machinery around 1779.]

RELATED WORD:
  noun — **Lud′dism**

46

mel·lif·lu·ous (mə-lĭf′lo͞o-əs)

adjective

Having a pleasant and fluid sound: *"The Headmaster read a rather lengthy passage from Stephen Vincent Benet's 'The Devil and Daniel Webster' in his engaging, mellifluous voice"* (John Knowles, *Peace Breaks Out*).

[Middle English, from Late Latin *mellifluus* : Latin *mel, mell-*, honey + Latin *-fluus*, flowing.]

RELATED WORDS:
    adverb—**mel·lif′lu·ous·ly**
    noun—**mel·lif′lu·ous·ness**

47

mi·as·ma (mī-ăz′mə, mē-ăz′mə)

noun

1. A harmful atmosphere or influence: *"The family affection, the family expectations, seemed to permeate the atmosphere . . . like a coiling miasma"* (Louis Auchincloss, *Honorable Men*). **2a.** A bad-smelling vapor arising from rotting organic matter and formerly thought to cause disease. **b.** A thick vaporous atmosphere or emanation: *wreathed in a miasma of cigarette smoke.*

[Greek, pollution, stain, from *miainein*, to pollute.]

They talked about their research grants. His, thanks to some long-deceased and long-forgotten zoologist called Vickery, was **munificent**. Hers was meagre. Was this discrimination, and if so, of what nature?

—Margaret Drabble
The Sea Lady

mu·nif·i·cent (myōō-nĭf′ĭ-sənt)

adjective

1. Very liberal in giving; generous: *a munificent bene-factor.* **2.** Characterized by great generosity or abundance: *"They talked about their research grants. His . . . was munificent. Hers was meagre."* (Margaret Drabble, *The Sea Lady*).

[Latin *mūnificēns, mūnificent-*, from *mūnificus* : *mūnus*, gift + *facere*, to make.]

RELATED WORDS:
> *noun* — **mu·nif′i·cence**
> *adverb* — **mu·nif′i·cent·ly**

49

na·scence (nā′səns, năs′əns)

noun

A coming into being; a beginning: *"The home market for grains, beef, and truck crops that developed directly out of the mining economy was the nascence of California agriculture"* (Julie Guthman, *Agrarian Dreams*).

[Latin *nāscentia*, birth.]

50

ne·o·phyte (nē′ə-fīt′)

noun

1. A recent convert to a belief. **2.** A beginner or novice: *a neophyte at politics.* **3a.** A newly ordained Roman Catholic priest. **b.** A novice of a religious order or congregation.

[Middle English *neophite*, from Late Latin *neophytus*, from Greek *neophutos*, newly planted, a recent convert : *neo-*, new + *-phutos*, planted (from *phuein*, to bring forth, make grow).]

nex·us (nĕk′səs)

noun
> Plural: **nexus** or **nex·us·es**

1. A means of connection; a link or tie: *"The first program in the series . . . explores the nexus between Latin Baroque and folk works"* (New York Times). **2.** A connected series or group: *"All three investigations focus to some extent on the nexus of politics, nonprofit groups and real estate developers in Brooklyn"* (William K. Rashbaum, *New York Times*). **3.** The core or center: *"The real nexus of the money culture [was] Wall Street"* (Bill Barol).

[Latin, from past participle of *nectere,* to bind.]

noi·some (noi′səm)

adjective

1. Offensive to the point of arousing disgust; foul: *There's a noisome odor coming from the garbage can.* **2.** Harmful or dangerous: *The paint gave off noisome fumes.*

[Middle English *noiesom* : *noie,* harm (short for *anoi,* annoyance, from Old French, from *anoier,* to annoy) + *-som,* adjectival suffix.]

RELATED WORDS:
> *adverb*—**noi′some·ly**
> *noun*—**noi′some·ness**

nom·i·nal (nŏm′ə-nəl)

adjective

1a. Existing in name only; not real: *"a person with a nominal religious position but no actual duties"* (Leo Damrosch, *Jean-Jacques Rousseau*). **b.** Insignificantly small; trifling: *a nominal sum.* **2a.** Resembling, relating to, or consisting of a name or names: *nominal aphasia.* **b.** Assigned to or bearing a person's name: *nominal shares.* **3.** *Philosophy* Relating to nominalism, the philosophical doctrine that general categories and qualities have no reality and exist only as names. **4.** *Economics* Relating to an amount or rate that is not adjusted for inflation. **5.** *Business* Relating to the face value of a security rather than the market value. **6.** *Grammar* Relating to a noun or word group that functions as a noun.

noun

Grammar A word or group of words functioning as a noun.

[Middle English *nominalle*, of nouns, from Latin *nōminālis*, of names, from *nōmen, nōmin-*, name.]

RELATED WORD:

    adverb **—nom′i·nal·ly**

o·bliq·ui·ty (ō-blĭk′wĭ-tē)

noun

Plural: **o·bliq·ui·ties**

1a. The quality or condition of being oblique, especially in deviating from a vertical or horizontal line, plane, position, or direction. **b.** The angle or extent of such a deviation. **2a.** Deviation from moral or proper conduct or thought: *"Eleanor did not believe that early rising could possibly be compatible with moral obliquity"* (Elizabeth Bowen, *Collected Stories*). **b.** An instance of this. **3.** Indirectness in conduct or verbal expression; lack of straightforwardness: *"It may be that the candor of contemporary literature creates a nostalgia for indirection, obliquity and deferral"* (Anatole Broyard, *New York Times Book Review*).

[From Middle French *obliquité*, from Latin *oblīquitāt-*, *oblīquitās*.]

RELATED WORD:

    adjective—**o·bliq′ui·tous**

on·tog·e·ny (ŏn-tŏj′ə-nē)

noun

Plural: **on·tog·e·nies**

The development of an individual organism or a part of an organism from inception to maturity: *the ontogeny of mammals; the ontogeny of the immune system.*

RELATED WORDS:
adjective—**on′to·ge·net′ic** (ŏn′tə-jə-nĕt′ĭk)
adverb—**on′to·ge·net′i·cal·ly**

op·pro·bri·um (ə-prō′brē-əm)

noun

1. Disgrace arising from exceedingly shameful conduct; ignominy: *The dictator's attacks on dissidents drew international opprobrium.* **2.** Scornful reproach or contempt: *a term of opprobrium.* **3.** *Archaic* A cause of shame or disgrace.

[Latin, from *opprobrāre*, to reproach : *ob-*, against + *probrum*, reproach.]

os·si·fy (ŏs′ə-fī′)

verb
> Past participle and past tense: **os·si·fied**
> Present participle: **os·si·fy·ing**
> Third person singular present tense: **os·si·fies**

intransitive: **1.** To change into bone; become bony. **2.** To become set in a rigidly conventional pattern: *"The central ideas of liberalism have ossified"* (Jeffrey Hart, *National Review*).

transitive: **1.** To convert (a membrane or cartilage, for example) into bone. **2.** To mold into a rigidly conventional pattern.

[Latin *os, oss-*, bone + English *–fy.*]

RELATED WORD:
> *adjective*—**os·sif′ic** (ŏ-sĭf′ĭk)

58

o·vip·a·rous (ō-vĭp′ər-əs)

adjective

Producing eggs that hatch outside the body: *Birds are oviparous.*

[Latin *ōviparus*, egg-laying.]

RELATED WORDS:
>   *noun* — **o′vi·par′i·ty** (ō′və-păr′ĭ-tē)
>   *adverb* — **o·vip′a·rous·ly**

59

pal·pa·ble (păl′pə-bəl)

adjective

1. Easily perceived; obvious: *"There was a palpable sense of expectation in the court"* (Nelson DeMille, *Word of Honor*). **2.** Capable of being handled, touched, or felt; tangible: *a palpable lymph node; a looming figure that was not a phantom but a palpable reality.*

[Middle English, from Old French, from Late Latin *palpābilis*, from Latin *palpāre*, to touch gently.]

RELATED WORD:
>   *adverb* — **pal′pa·bly**

pan·o·ply (păn′ə-plē)

noun
Plural: **pan·o·plies**

1. An impressive or striking array or arrangement: *"The new information could . . . help astronomers understand the panoply of Earth-size planets around other stars and the possibility of conditions friendly for life on them"* (Kenneth Chang, *New York Times*). **2.** Ceremonial attire with all accessories: *a portrait of the general in full panoply.* **3.** The complete arms and armor of a warrior.

[Greek *panopliā* : *pan-*, all + *hopla*, arms, armor, plural of *hoplon*, weapon.]

pe·nu·ri·ous (pə-nŏŏr′ē-əs)

adjective

1. Poverty-stricken; destitute. **2.** Unwilling to spend money; stingy: *a penurious miser.* **3.** Scanty or meager: *"an allowance of cold meat and bread, in the same penurious proportion observed in our ordinary meals"* (Charlotte Brontë, *Jane Eyre*).

[From Medieval Latin *pēnūriōsus*, from Latin *pēnūria*, want.]

RELATED WORDS:

    adverb—**pe·nu′ri·ous·ly**
    noun—**pe·nu′ri·ous·ness**

Sundays were dreary days in that wintry season. We had to walk two miles to Brocklebridge Church, where our patron officiated. We set out cold, we arrived at church colder: during the morning service we became almost paralysed. It was too far to return to dinner, and an allowance of cold meat and bread, in the same **penurious** proportion observed in our ordinary meals, was served round between the services.

—Charlotte Brontë
Jane Eyre

per·mu·ta·tion (pûr′myŏo-tā′shən)

noun

1. A rearrangement of the elements of a group or set. For example, the permutations of the set composed of *x, y,* and *z* are *xyz, xzy, yxz, yzx, zxy, zyx.* **2.** A complete change; a transformation: *the country's permutation into a modern democracy.*

[Middle English *permutacioun,* exchange of something for another, Latin *permūtātiōn-, permūtātiō,* exchange, transposition.]

RELATED WORD:

    adjective—**per′mu·ta′tion·al**

per·pe·tu·i·ty (pûr′pĭ-tōō′ĭ-tē)

noun

1. The quality or condition of being eternal: *"The perpetuity of the Church was an article of faith"* (Morris L. West). **2.** Time without end; eternity.

IDIOM:

in perpetuity For an indefinite period of time; forever: *According to her will, the lands of her estate were donated to the city for use as a public park in perpetuity.*

[Middle English *perpetuite*, from Latin *perpetuitāt-*, *perpetuitās*, temporal or spatial continuity, from Latin *perpetuus*, permanent.]

per·qui·site (pûr′kwĭ-zĭt)

noun

1. A payment, profit, or benefit received in addition to a regular wage or salary, especially when due or expected: *Free use of a car was one of the supervisor's perquisites.*
2. Something regarded or claimed as an exclusive right by virtue of one's social position or rank: *"The family had the perquisites of the upper-middle class, employing a maid, a chauffeur-gardener, and an Irish Catholic nanny"* (Ira Bruce Nadel, *Various Positions: A Life of Leonard Cohen*).

[From Middle English *perquisites*, property acquired otherwise than by inheritance, from Medieval Latin *perquīsītum*, acquisition, from Latin, neuter past participle of *perquīrere*, to search diligently for : *per-*, thoroughly + *quaerere*, to seek.]

pha·lanx (fā′lăngks′, făl′ăngks′)

noun
Plural: **pha·lanx·es** or **pha·lan·ges** (fə-lăn′jēz, fā-lăn′jēz)

1. A compact gathering of people: *a solid phalanx of demonstrators on the capitol steps.* **2.** In ancient Greece, a formation of infantry carrying overlapping shields and long spears. **3.** *Plural:* **phalanges** A bone of a finger or toe.

[Latin *phalanx*, *phalang-*, from Greek.]

pla·ce·bo (plə-sē′bō)

noun

Plural: **pla·ce·bos** or **pla·ce·boes**

1. A substance that has positive effects on a patient's health as a result of the patient's perception that it is beneficial rather than as a result of a causative ingredient. **2.** An inactive substance or preparation used as a control in an experiment or test to determine the effectiveness of a medicinal drug. **3.** Something of no intrinsic remedial value that is used to appease or reassure another. **4.** (plä-chä′bō) *Roman Catholic Church* The service or office of vespers for the dead.

[Latin *placēbō*, I shall please, first person singular future tense of Latin *placēre*, to please. Sense 4, from Late Latin *placēbō*, I shall please, the first word of the first antiphon of the vespers service.]

WORD HISTORY **Placebo** has its origin in the Office of the Dead, the cycle of prayers traditionally sung or recited for the repose of the souls of the dead. The traditional liturgical language of the Roman Catholic Church is Latin, and in Latin, the first word of the first antiphon of the vespers service is *placēbō*, "I shall please." This word is taken from a phrase in the psalm text that is recited after the antiphon, *placēbō Dominō in regiōne vīvōrum*, "I shall please the Lord in the land of the living." The vespers service of the Office of the Dead came to be called *placebo* in Middle English, and the expression *sing placebo* came to mean "to flatter, be obsequious." *Placebo* eventually came to mean "flatterer" and "sycophant." In the 1700s, *placebo* began to be used of prescriptions written by a physician solely to please a patient, as by satisfying the patient's desire to take medicine. In many cases, the patient would actually benefit, thanks to what became known as the *placebo effect*. Later, *placebo* came to refer to neutral substances used in controlled studies testing the effectiveness of medications.

prox·i·mate (prŏk′sə-mĭt)

adjective

1. Direct or immediate: *"The stock market crash in October, 1929 . . . is often regarded as . . . the major proximate cause of the Great Depression"* (Milton Friedman, *Capitalism and Freedom*). **2.** Very near or next, as in space, time, or order.

[Latin *proximātus*, past participle of *proximāre*, to come near, from *proximus*, nearest.]

RELATED WORD:
    adverb—**prox′i·mate·ly**

quer·u·lous (kwĕr′ə-ləs)

adjective

1. Given to complaining; peevish: *The querulous customers demanded to see the manager.* **2.** Expressing a complaint or grievance; grumbling: *The blog post received many querulous comments.*

[Middle English *querulose*, litigious, quarrelsome, from Old French *querelos*, from Late Latin *querulōsus*, querulous, from Latin *querulus*, from *querī*, to complain.]

RELATED WORDS:
    adverb—**quer′u·lous·ly**
    noun—**quer′u·lous·ness**

quo·rum (kwôr′əm)

noun

The minimal number of officers and members of a committee or organization, usually a majority, who must be present for valid transaction of business.

[Middle English, quorum of justices of the peace, from Latin *quōrum*, of whom (from the wording of a commission naming certain persons as members of a body), genitive plural of *quī*, who.]

ra·pa·cious (rə-pā′shəs)

adjective

1. Having or showing a strong or excessive desire to acquire money or possess things; greedy: *"dishonest utilities and rapacious energy traders"* (Paul Roberts, *The End of Oil*). **2.** Living by killing prey, especially in large numbers: *rapacious coyotes.* **3.** Taking things by force; plundering: *rapacious pirates.*

[From Latin *rapāx, rapāc-*, from *rapere*, to seize.]

RELATED WORDS:
>   *adverb*—**ra·pa′cious·ly**
>   *noun*—**ra·pac′i·ty** (rə-păs′ĭ-tē), **ra·pa′cious·ness**

re·frac·to·ry (rĭ-frăk′tə-rē)

adjective

1. Showing or characterized by obstinate resistance to authority or control: *refractory children; refractory behavior.* **2.** Difficult to melt or work; resistant to heat: *a refractory material such as silica.* **3.** Resistant to treatment: *a refractory case of acne.*

[Alteration (influenced by adjectives in *–ory*) of obsolete *refractary*, from Latin *refrāctārius*, from *refrāctus*, past participle of *refringere*, to break up.]

RELATED WORDS:
>   *adverb*—**re·frac′to·ri·ly**
>   *noun*—**re·frac′to·ri·ness**

re·pu·di·ate (rĭ-pyōō'dē-āt')

transitive verb

Past participle and past tense: **re·pu·di·at·ed**
Present participle: **re·pu·di·at·ing**
Third person singular present tense: **re·pu·di·ates**

1. To reject the validity or authority of: *"The first great poet in the English language, Chaucer, not only came to doubt the worth of his extraordinary body of work, but repudiated it"* (Joyce Carol Oates, *(Woman) Writer*). **2.** To reject emphatically as unfounded, untrue, or unjust: *repudiated the accusation.* **3.** To refuse to recognize or pay: *repudiate a debt.*

[Latin *repudiāre, repudiāt-*, from *repudium*, divorce.]

RELATED WORDS:
adjective—**re·pu'di·a'tive**
noun—**re·pu'di·a'tor**

ris·i·ble (rĭz′ə-bəl)

adjective

1. Eliciting laughter; ludicrous: *"When we first bought the farm, I used to take a chair outside in the summer sun and watch the water move. My Canadian friends thought it a risible thing to do. Water was water, and it was everywhere, wasn't it?"* (Marq de Villiers, *Water*).
2. Relating to laughter or used in laughing: *the risible muscles of the face.*

[Late Latin *rīsibilis*, from Latin *rīsus*, past participle of *rīdēre*, to laugh.]

RELATED WORDS:
       noun — **ris′i·bil′i·ty** (rĭz′ə-bĭl′ĭ-tē)
       adverb — **ris′i·bly**

When we first bought the farm, I used to take a chair outside in the summer sun and watch the water move. My Canadian friends thought it a **risible** thing to do. Water was water, and it was everywhere, wasn't it? I paid no attention, but stared down at the little spring. It bubbled and seeped and gurgled, and it was cold when I reached down to touch it. I had never "owned" water before. I grew up in the arid center of the South African plains. It hardly rained there (though when it did, the clouds burst), and for most of the year the rivers were dry, dusty places where thorn bushes grew and weaver-birds made their nests.

—Marq de Villiers
Water

sa·li·ent (sā′lē-ənt)

adjective

1. Noteworthy; important: *repeated the salient points of the argument.* **2.** Prominent; conspicuous: *The bell tower is the most salient feature on campus.* **3.** Projecting beyond a line or surface: *the salient angles of the polygon.* **4.** Springing; jumping: *salient tree toads.*

noun

1. A military position that projects into the position of the enemy. **2.** A projecting angle or part.

[Latin *saliēns, salient-,* present participle of *salīre,* to leap.]

RELATED WORD:
  adverb — **sa′li·ent·ly**

sanc·ti·mo·ni·ous (săngk′tə-mō′nē-əs)

adjective

1. Behaving with smug or hypocritical righteousness: *We got tired of sanctimonious people lecturing us about the healthy foods we should be eating.* **2.** Characterized by smug or hypocritical righteousness: *The article was nothing but a sanctimonious condemnation of other people's behavior.*

[From Latin *sānctimōnia,* sacredness, from *sānctus,* holy.]

RELATED WORDS:
  adverb — **sanc′ti·mo′ni·ous·ly**
  noun — **sanc′ti·mo′ni·ous·ness**

sar·don·ic (sär-dŏn′ĭk)

adjective

1. Scornfully or cynically mocking: *"He is slight in stature, with a mop of puffy brown hair that always seems to have a runaway cowlick and a sardonic sneer that he uses [to] convey a comedic level of disbelief"* (Rachel Syme, *Time.com*). **2.** Given to making scornful or cynically mocking remarks: *The actor plays a sardonic young man who never takes anything seriously.*

[French *sardonique*, from Greek *sardonios*.]

RELATED WORDS:
> *adverb* — **sar·don′i·cal·ly**
> *noun* — **sar·don′i·cism** (sär-dŏn′ĭ-sĭz′əm)

scur·ri·lous (skûr′ə-ləs)

adjective

1. Expressed in vulgar, coarse, or abusive language: *a scurrilous screed against government intrusion.* **2.** Malicious or slanderous in nature; defamatory: *"The law affords them wide First Amendment protection . . . even when they write scurrilous lies"* (Richard Curtis, *How To Be Your Own Literary Agent*). **3.** Given to the use of vulgar, coarse, or abusive language: *accused him of being a scurrilous rogue.*

[*scurrile* (from French *scurrile*, from Latin *scurrīlis*, jeering, from Latin *scurra*, buffoon) + *-ous*.]

RELATED WORDS:
 adverb — **scur′ri·lous·ly**
 noun — **scur′ri·lous·ness**

se·ques·ter (sĭ-kwĕs′tər)

transitive verb

Past participle and past tense: **se·ques·tered**
Present participle: **se·ques·ter·ing**
Third person singular present tense: **se·ques·ters**

1. To remove or set apart; segregate: *sequester a jury.*
2. To remove (oneself or another) from the company of others by withdrawing to a private or isolated place: *"Some of the actors . . . found it disturbing that the director was sequestered in an off-stage control booth"* (Gene D. Phillips, *Godfather*). **3.** To remove or isolate (a chemical, often a gas) from an environment by incorporation, mixing, or insertion under pressure: *plants that sequester toxins from wetlands; plans to sequester carbon dioxide produced by a power plant by injection into an underground aquifer.* **4.** To take possession of (property) until a legal claim is settled.

[Middle English *sequestren,* from Old French, from Latin *sequestrāre,* to give up for safekeeping, from Latin *sequester,* depositary, trustee.]

Sis·y·phe·an (sĭs′ə-fē′ən)

adjective

1. Relating to Sisyphus. In Greek mythology, Sisyphus was the cruel king of Corinth who was condemned to repeatedly roll a huge stone up a hill in Hades, only to have it roll down again each time he neared the top. **2.** Endlessly laborious or futile: *"The jumble of wet pans and platters . . . made him weary; to dry them seemed a task as Sisyphean as to repair the things wrong with his parents' house"* (Jonathan Franzen, *The Corrections*).

[From Latin *Sisyphēius*, from Greek *Sisupheios*, from *Sisuphos*, Sisyphus.]

so·lic·i·tous (sə-lĭs′ĭ-təs)

adjective

1. Showing great attention to another: *a solicitous parent; solicitous for your welfare; solicitous of his young sister.* **2.** Expressing concern for another: *made solicitous inquiries about our family.* **3.** Showing great care; careful or meticulous: *"Every thing that . . . the most solicitous care could do to render her comfortable, was the office of each watchful companion"* (Jane Austen, *Sense and Sensibility*).

[Latin *sollicitus* : *sollus*, entire + *citus*, past participle of *ciēre*, to set in motion.]

RELATED WORDS:
> *adverb*—**so·lic′i·tous·ly**
> *noun*—**so·lic′i·tous·ness**

The Dashwoods were two days on the road, and Marianne bore her journey on both, without essential fatigue. Every thing that the most zealous affection, the most **solicitous** care could do to render her comfortable, was the office of each watchful companion, and each found their reward in her bodily ease, and her calmness of spirits.

—Jane Austen
Sense and Sensibility

sub·sume (səb-sōōm′)

transitive verb

    Past participle and past tense: **sub·sumed**
    Present participle: **sub·sum·ing**
    Third person singular present tense: **sub·sumes**

1. To classify or include in a more comprehensive category or under a general principle: *"When late eighteenth-century Americans spoke of politics, they referred to a broad set of principles that they subsumed under the heading of republicanism"* (Eric Foner, *The New American History*). **2.** To absorb (something) into or cause (something) to be overshadowed by something else: *"The moment's regret was subsumed in the needs of the next moment"* (Diana Gabaldon, *An Echo in the Bone*).

[Medieval Latin *subsūmere* : Latin *sub-*, under + Latin *sūmere*, to take.]

RELATED WORD:
    adjective — **sub·sum′a·ble**

te·na·cious (tə-nā′shəs)

adjective

1. Extremely persistent in adhering to or doing something; stubborn: *"tenacious defenders of their harsh and pitiless land"* (Dee Brown, *Bury My Heart at Wounded Knee*). **2.** Characterized by extreme persistence; relentless or enduring: *tenacious detective work; tenacious superstitions.* **3.** Tending to retain; retentive: *a tenacious memory.*

[From Latin *tenāx, tenāc-*, holding fast, from *tenēre*, to hold.]

RELATED WORDS:
> *adverb* — **te·na′cious·ly**
> *noun* — **te·nac′i·ty** (tə-năs′ĭ-tē), **te·na′cious·ness**

🦉 **WORD HISTORY** The word root *ten-* in English words comes from the Latin verb *tenēre*, "to hold." The word **tenacious,** for example, comes from this verb by way of the Latin adjective *tenāc-*, "holding fast, persistent." The Latin word root *ten-* often has the form *tain-* in French, and English has words from both forms. A *tenant* is one "holding land from a lord or holding something on lease." To *retain* is "to keep back, keep possession of" (*re-*, "back").

trav·es·ty (trăv′ĭ-stē)

noun
Plural: **trav·es·ties**

1. A debased or grotesque likeness: *rigged elections that were a travesty of democracy.* **2.** An exaggerated or grotesque imitation, such as a parody of a literary work.

transitive verb
Past participle and past tense: **trav·es·tied**
Present participle: **trav·es·ty·ing**
Third person singular present tense: **trav·es·ties**

To make a travesty of; parody or ridicule: *The author has travestied the original poem.*

[From obsolete English *travesty*, disguised, burlesqued, from French *travesti*, past participle of *travestir*, to disguise, parody, from Italian *travestire* : Latin *trāns-*, across + Latin *vestīre*, to dress (from *vestis*, garment).]

tri·age (trē-äzh′, trē′äzh′)

noun

1. A process for sorting injured people into groups based on their need for or likely benefit from immediate medical treatment. Triage is used in hospital emergency rooms, on battlefields, and at disaster sites when limited medical resources must be allocated. **2.** A system used to allocate a scarce commodity, such as food, only to those capable of deriving the greatest benefit from it. **3.** A process in which things are ranked in terms of importance or priority: *"For millions of Americans, each week becomes a stressful triage between work and home that leaves them feeling guilty, exhausted and angry"* (Jill Smolowe, *Time*).

transitive verb

 Past participle and past tense: **tri·aged**
 Present participle: **tri·ag·ing**
 Third person singular present tense: **tri·ag·es**

To sort or allocate by triage: *triaged the patients according to their symptoms.*

[French, from *trier*, to sort, from Old French, to pick out.]

truc·u·lent (trŭk′yə-lənt)

adjective

1. Ready or willing to fight; belligerent: *Truculent fans started yelling and running out on the playing field.* **2.** Showing or expressing bitter opposition or hostility; aggressively defiant: *a truculent speech against the new government; a truculent glance.*

[Latin *truculentus,* from *trux, truc-,* fierce.]

RELATED WORDS:

> *noun*—**truc′u·lence** (trŭk′yə-ləns), **truc′u·len·cy** (trŭk′yə-lən-sē)
> *adverb*—**truc′u·lent·ly**

um·brage (ŭm′brĭj)

noun

1. Offense or resentment: *"On one occasion her insults had been so brilliant and finely calculated that the groom took umbrage and cancelled the wedding"* (Salman Rushdie, *Midnight's Children*). **2.** *Archaic* Shadow or shade: *"the Red Maple . . . with its cool, deep, yet not oppressive umbrage"* (Donald Culross Peattie, *A Natural History of North American Trees*).

[Middle English, shade, from Old French, from Latin *umbrāticum,* neuter of *umbrāticus,* of shade, from *umbra,* shadow.]

un·re·gen·er·ate (ŭn′rĭ-jĕn′ər-ĭt)

adjective

1. Not spiritually or morally reformed; unrepentant: *an unregenerate sinner.* **2.** Persistently unwilling to accept change; obstinate: *"a senator who had been an unregenerate foe to woman suffrage"* (Lillian Faderman, *To Believe in Woman*).

[*un-* + *regenerate* (Latin *regenerāre, regenerāt-,* to reproduce).]

RELATED WORDS:
> *adjective*—**un′re·gen′er·a·ble**
> *noun*—**un′re·gen′er·a·cy** (ŭn′rĭ-jĕn′ər-ə-sē)
> *adverb*—**un′re·gen′er·ate·ly**

un·ten·a·ble (ŭn-tĕn′ə-bəl)

adjective

1. Not capable of being maintained or defended: *an untenable political argument; an untenable situation.* **2.** Not capable of being occupied or lived in: *untenable living quarters.*

[*un-* + *tenable* (from Old French *tenir,* to hold, from Latin *tenēre*).]

RELATED WORDS:
> *noun*—**un·ten′a·bil′i·ty, un·ten′a·ble·ness**
> *adverb*—**un·ten′a·bly**

u·su·ry (yoॊo'zhə-rē)

noun

Plural: **u·su·ries**

1. The practice of lending money and charging the borrower interest, especially at an exorbitant or illegally high rate. **2.** An excessive or illegally high rate of interest charged on borrowed money. **3.** *Archaic* Interest charged or paid on a loan.

[Middle English, from Medieval Latin *ūsūria*, alteration of Latin *ūsūra*, from *ūsus*, use.]

ver·i·si·mil·i·tude (věr'ə-sĭ-mĭl'ĭ-toॊod')

noun

The quality of appearing to be true or real: *"The painting owes its verisimilitude to a number of groundbreaking innovations. Its life-size figures are rendered with a new kind of sculptural modeling, which makes them seem to occupy real space"* (Jack Flam, *Wall Street Journal*).

[Latin *vērīsimilitūdō*, from *vērīsimilis*, verisimilar (*vērī*, genitive of *vērum*, truth + *similis*, similar).]

RELATED WORD:

　　　adjective—**ver'i·si·mil'i·tu'di·nous** (věr'ə-sĭ-mĭl'ĭ-toॊod'n-əs)

ver·nac·u·lar (vər-năk′yə-lər)

noun

1. The ordinary spoken language of a country or locality as distinct from the literary language. **2.** The specialized vocabulary of a particular trade, profession, or group: *in the legal vernacular.*

adjective

1. Native to or commonly spoken by the members of a particular country or region: *a folk tale told in a vernacular dialect.* **2.** Using the native language of a region, especially as distinct from the literary language: *a vernacular poet.* **3.** Designating the common, nonscientific name of a biological species: *The vernacular name of* Quercus alba *is "white oak."*

[From Latin *vernāculus,* native, from *verna,* native slave, perhaps of Etruscan origin.]

RELATED WORD:
        adverb—**ver·nac′u·lar·ly**

ver·tig·i·nous (vər-tĭj′ə-nəs)

adjective

1. Tending to produce dizziness or disorientation because of rapid change or great height: *driving on windy, vertiginous roads; the vertiginous growth of the computer industry.* **2.** Affected by vertigo; dizzy: *Looking over the edge of the cliff, I suddenly felt vertiginous.* **3.** Turning about an axis; revolving or whirling: *the vertiginous motion of the earth.*

[From Latin *vertīgō, vertīgin-*, a whirling, from *vertere*, to turn.]

RELATED WORDS:
　　adverb—**ver·tig′i·nous·ly**
　　noun—**ver·tig′i·nous·ness**

vo·cif·er·ous (vō-sĭf′ər-əs)

adjective

Making, given to, or marked by noisy and vehement outcry: *"a long line of gentlemen . . . uttering vociferous cheers"* (Charles Dickens, *The Life and Adventures of Nicholas Nickleby*).

[Latin *vocifer(ārī)*, to speak loudly + *-ous*.]

RELATED WORDS:
　　adverb—**vo·cif′er·ous·ly**
　　noun—**vo·cif′er·ous·ness**

Several very exciting skirmishes were in progress, when a loud shout attracted the attention even of the belligerents, and then there poured on to the platform, from a door at the side, a long line of gentlemen with their hats off, all looking behind them, and uttering **vociferous** cheers.

—Charles Dickens
The Life and Adventures of Nicholas Nickleby

wel·ter (wĕl′tər)

noun

1. A confused mass; a jumble: *a welter of papers and magazines.* **2.** Confusion; turmoil.

intransitive verb

  Past participle and past tense: **wel·tered**
  Present participle: **wel·ter·ing**
  Third person singular present tense: **wel·ters**

1. To wallow, roll, or toss about, as in mud or high seas.
2. To lie soaked in a liquid.

[From Middle English *welteren*, to toss about, as in high seas, from Middle Low German or Middle Dutch, to roll.]

wi·ki (wĭk′ē)

noun
> Plural: **wi·kis**

A collaborative website whose content can be edited by anyone who has access to it.

[Originally an abbreviation of *WikiWikiWeb*, software developed by American computer programmer Howard G. Cunningham (born 1949) : Hawaiian *wikiwiki*, very quick (akin to Tahitian *viti, vitiviti*, deft) + *web*.]

WORD HISTORY A **wiki** is a collaborative website whose content can be edited by anyone with access to it, and the word *wiki* is a good example of how the invention of new technologies requires the invention of new words. *Wiki* is short for *WikiWikiWeb*, the name that American computer programmer Howard G. Cunningham chose in 1995 for his new code permitting the easy development of collaborative websites. He coined the word *WikiWikiWeb* from Hawaiian *wikiwiki*, meaning "very quick" (*wiki* by itself means "fast, quick"), with the thought that *WikiWikiWeb* was more fun to say than "quick web." *Wikiwiki* was the first native Hawaiian word that Cunningham learned when he visited the islands. When the airport counter agent told him to take the "wikiwiki bus" between terminals, he asked what that meant. The agent explained that *wikiwiki* meant "quick." From that first chance encounter, a local Hawaiian word became part of the global lexicon.

win·some (wĭn′səm)

adjective

Charming, often in a childlike or naive way.

[Middle English *winsum*, from Old English *wynsum* : from *wynn*, joy + *-sum*, characterized by.]

RELATED WORDS:

> *adverb* — **win′some·ly**
> *noun* — **win′some·ness**

🐚 **WORD HISTORY** The *win* in **winsome** comes from the Indo-European root **wen–*, meaning "to desire, strive for," and has a number of descendants in the Germanic languages. One was the prehistoric Germanic noun **wini–* meaning "friend" (literally, "one who desires or loves" someone else), which became *wine* in Old English and is preserved in such names as *Winfred,* "friend of peace," and *Edwin,* "friend of (family) possessions." A different form of the root with a different suffix became Old English *wynn,* "pleasure, joy," preserved in *winsome*. Finally, the verb *win* itself is from this root; its meaning is an extension of the sense "to strive for," namely, "to strive for with success, be victorious." Outside of the Germanic branch of Indo-European, we see the root, for example, in Latin *venus* or *Venus* "love, the goddess of love," and the verb *venerāre,* "to worship," the source of English *venerate*.

xer·ic (zĕr′ĭk)

adjective

Relating to, characterized by, or adapted to an extremely dry habitat: *a botanist who studies xeric woodlands; xeric mosses that can survive long periods without rain.*

[From Greek *xēros*, dry.]

RELATED WORDS:
    adverb — **xer′i·cal·ly**
    noun — **xe·ric′i·ty** (zĕ-rĭs′ĭ-tē)

yaw (yô)

intransitive verb

Past participle and past tense: **yawed**
Present participle: **yaw·ing**
Third person singular present tense: **yaws**

1. To swerve off course momentarily or temporarily: *The schooner yawed in the rough seas.* **2.** To turn right or left about a vertical axis: *The plane yawed because of the strong wind.*

noun

1. The act of yawing. **2.** Extent of yawing, measured in degrees: *The pilot corrected for the yaw of the plane.*

[Perhaps of Scandinavian origin.]

99

ze·ro-sum (zîr′ō-sŭm′)

adjective

Relating to a situation in which a gain is offset by an equal loss: *"Under the zero-sum budgeting system that governs federal spending, the money for spinal research is likely to be deducted from some other research account"* (Daniel S. Greenburg, *Washington Post*).

100

zy·gote (zī′gōt′)

noun

The cell formed by the union of two gametes, especially a fertilized egg cell.

[From Greek *zugōtos*, yoked, from *zugoun*, to yoke.]

RELATED WORD:
  adjective — **zy·got′ic** (zī-gŏt′ĭk)

The 100 Words

alacrity
amorphous
anathema
anomie
antithesis
apotheosis
arcanum
bathos
bellwether
bespeak
caldera
coalesce
compunction
conflate
crepuscular
cynosure
debunk
derivative
diaphanous
duress
efface
effulgent
eponymous
eureka
excoriate
fastidious
feint
feral
gaffe
galvanize
gravitas
habiliments
heterodox
hydrocarbon

impugn
inchoate
indigenous
innate
intransigent
juggernaut
kelvin
lacuna
lambent
lineament
Luddite
mellifluous
miasma
munificent
nascence
neophyte
nexus
noisome
nominal
obliquity
ontogeny
opprobrium
ossify
oviparous
palpable
panoply
penurious
permutation
perpetuity
perquisite
phalanx
placebo
proximate
querulous

quorum
rapacious
refractory
repudiate
risible
salient
sanctimonious
sardonic
scurrilous
sequester
Sisyphean
solicitous
subsume
tenacious
travesty
triage
truculent
umbrage
unregenerate
untenable
usury
verisimilitude
vernacular
vertiginous
vociferous
welter
wiki
winsome
xeric
yaw
zero-sum
zygote

Other Books in THE 100 WORDS® Series

From the editors of *The American Heritage® Dictionary of the English Language*, 5th Edition